INTERACT

YARD

Paul Cheshire

SERIES CONSULTANT: LORRAINE PETERSEN

RISING STARS

nasen
Helping Everyone Achieve

NASEN House, 4/5 Amber Business Village, Amber Close, Amington,
Tamworth, Staffordshire B77 4RP

Rising Stars UK Ltd.
22 Grafton Street, London W1S 4EX
www.risingstars-uk.com

Published 2009

Cover design: Burville-Riley Partnership
Illustrator: Dave Neale for Advocate Art
Text design and typesetting: Andy Wilson for Green Desert Ltd.
Publisher: Gill Budgell
Editor: Catherine Gilhooly
Series consultant: Lorraine Petersen

British Library Cataloguing in Publication Data.
A CIP record for this book is available from the British Library

ISBN 978-1-84680-502-8

Printed by Craft Print International Limited, Singapore

CONTENTS

CHARACTERS

Jamal

Lee's best friend. He loves computers and gadgets.

Lee

Jamal's best friend. He's into computers and gadgets too.

Jason

A cyber-bully and Claire's twin brother.

Characters

Claire

Jason's twin sister. She helps Jason to bully other people.

Mr McManus

The head teacher.

Narrator

The narrator tells the story.

You are logged on to: Yard
User Name:Jamal
Food Tube
You are logged on to: Yard
User Name: Lee
Food Tube

Scene 1

THE HACKER STRIKES!

Narrator It is lunchtime in 2050. Two friends, Lee and Jamal, are in a school of the future. They don't have classrooms. Instead, they use tiny computers on an armband.

Future schools don't have real playgrounds. Instead, children use a virtual reality world called Yard. Yard lets them swap pictures, music and jokes, or just chat.

Jamal Ah, that's better!
I was starting to lose it in there.

Lee In Mr Vee's maths class?

Jamal Yeah man! He's *so* boring!

Narrator Jamal waves his hand
in front of his screen.
The display switches
from 'Maths' to 'Yard'.

Lee Maybe bring ear plugs next time.

Jamal Yeah, I might do!

Narrator The boys are sitting next to each other
on exercise bikes. They chat
to their friends on Yard
and keep fit at the same time!

Lee I'm feeling hungry.

Narrator Lee speaks into his armband.

Lee What's for lunch today?

Narrator A screen pops up flashing the word 'EAT'. Then robots fill the screen showing a choice of food.

Lee Hmmm, baked potato and, erm ...

Jamal They got any pizza?
Get me one will you?

Lee Salad?

Jamal Go on then, extra tomatoes please.

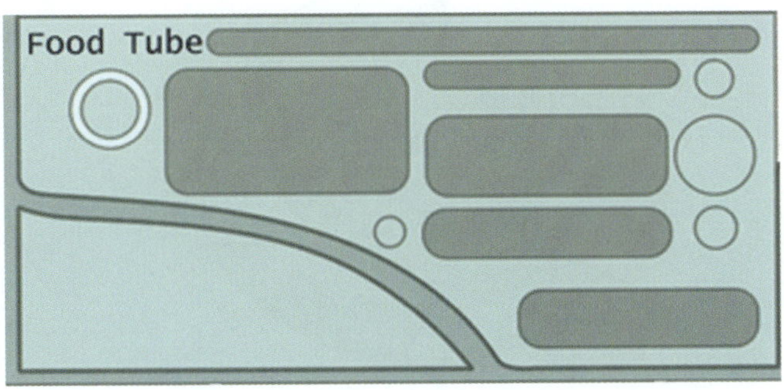

Narrator Lee and Jamal eat their meals
as they watch their screens.
They are swapping music files
with their friends. Then two new people
enter the Yard chatroom.

Jamal Uh-oh!

Lee On no man, not them!

Narrator It's the cyber-bully Jason
and his twin sister Claire.

Jamal Jason's *so* annoying, isn't he?

Narrator The screen blinks and flashes. Jason uploads a photograph of him and Claire. They are sitting in a brand new hover car.

Lee He's such a show-off!

Jamal Look at that car! It must have cost a fortune.

Lee They're always on our screens with their big cheesy grins!

Jamal Yeah, I've seen them both in other photos. They always have the latest gadgets.

Lee What a pair of show-offs!

Narrator Lee is sending a message to Jamal when a light flashes on his screen.

Lee Oh no! Hacker!!!

Narrator Jamal looks at his screen. Their chat is being hacked by Jason and Claire.

Jamal It's Jason and Claire.

Lee How do you know it's them?

Jamal I've heard other people complain about them hacking chats before. There's all sorts of kit you can buy to do it ... if you have the money.

Lee Yeah, I guess hacking isn't that hard if you have the right gadgets.
Hang on, what's going on?

Narrator A new version of Lee and Jamal's chat pops up on the screens.
It can be read by anyone else online.
Jamal reads the message aloud.

Jamal "Mr McManus is a ..."
Oh no!

Narrator Lee reads it too.

Lee Oh no! They can't do that!
We never wrote that!

Jamal Mr McManus is going to kill us!

Narrator The boys panic.
Then their screens suddenly go blank.

Lee What's going on?

Jamal Uh-oh. It's Mr McManus.

Mr McManus
Come to my office after school.

Jamal Ooohhhhh!

Lee Ooooh!

Narrator Jason and Claire look at their screens and laugh. They have hacked into Lee and Jamal's files and seen the head teacher's message.

Jason They are in *so* much trouble!

Claire Yeah, *big* trouble!

Jason McManus won't believe they didn't write that.

Claire Totally. He's too stupid to know we can hack into anybody's chat.

Jason Yeah, we can do what we like ...
to whoever we don't like!

Claire Nice one, Jase. We make trouble,
but we are never *in* trouble!

Jason and Claire (*together*)
Ha, ha, ha!

Head
Teacher's
Office
User Name: Mr. McManus

Scene 2

PUNISHED!

Narrator The boys meet up after school. They log onto the head teacher's office screen. The clock in the corner of the screen ticks slowly and loudly. Lee and Jamal wait nervously for Mr McManus to appear.

Lee I don't believe this! That Jason and his muppet sister!

Jamal We are in so much trouble!

Lee I know! But ...

Jamal But we didn't do anything!
It's not fair, it's not right!

Lee I wish I could get my hands on those two!

Jamal And then what?
You'd be in even more trouble.

Lee Hmmm, well ...

Jamal Anyway, that Jason looks pretty tough.

Narrator Lee tries to look tough.

Lee Well, I can be pretty tough
when I have to be.

Jamal Yeah, right!

Lee What?

Jamal As tough as a cup of tea!

Lee Okay, fair point.

Narrator Mr McManus appears. He looks at each boy and shakes his head.

Mr McManus
Ah, the two jokers!
I've been expecting you.

Lee But sir, that wasn't us.

Mr McManus
Do I look stupid?

Jamal Erm ...

Mr McManus
I said, do I look stupid? Well?

Jamal Do *you* look stupid, sir?

Lee What Jamal means sir is ... erm ...
of course you don't look stupid.
How could you? You're a teacher.

Jamal Ahem! Yes. The head of all the teachers.

Lee Which ... erm ... which makes you
the erm ... the least ...

Jamal The least stupid ... ?

Mr McManus
I beg your pardon?

Lee and Jamal (*together*)
Nothing sir, sorry sir.

Mr McManus
I can see you two think you are funny.
Well, let's see if you find this funny.
You must each write an essay on
'Why I am not cool or funny'.

Narrator The boys gulp quietly.

Mr McManus

And if I am not happy with your essays, you will do them again. And again, and again ... until I am happy.
I want them by tomorrow.

Narrator The screen goes blank.

Lee and Jamal (*together*)

Oh no!

Narrator Then Mr McManus returns to the screen. He is looking very pleased.

Mr McManus

Plus three weeks of cyber-detention.

Narrator The screen goes blank again.

Lee It's so unfair.

Jamal Yeah, totally. This is going to be so bad!

Narrator Over the next three weeks, people at school make fun of Lee and Jamal for the trouble they're in. They get lots of mean emails but a few friends are on their side. They know that it was all down to Jason and Claire's cyber-bullying tricks.

Jason Look at this photo of Jamal. I've added some text to it.

Claire What does it say? "I'm an idiot". Ha, ha, ha!

Jason And I've done this one for Lee.

Claire "I smell"... That's so funny!

Jason I know. I'm *so* clever.
I'm going to upload these photos
onto Yard so everyone can see them.

Claire Nice one, Jase. Are you sure the teachers
won't know who uploaded them?

Jason No way. We can log on to Yard
with a fake name.

Claire Sounds good to me.
Jamal and Lee are such losers.

Jason Totally. And they're doing
loser detention right now!

You are logged on to: Yard
User Name:Jamal
Food Tube
You are logged on to: Yard
User Name: Lee
Food Tube
You are logged on to: Yard
Lee: Here are the answers
to next week's test.
User Name: Lee

Head Teacher's Office
User Name:Mr.McManu

Jason's Homework
$c = mx^2$
$x = \sqrt{\frac{c}{m}}$
$c = ax^2 + bx$
$x^2 + \frac{b}{a}x = \frac{c}{a}$

You are logged on to: Yard
Lee: Here are the answers to next week's test.
User Name: Lee

Scene 3

THE HACKER STRIKES AGAIN!

Narrator Lee and Jamal have finished their three weeks of cyber-detention. Lee is messaging Jamal who is in another room.

Lee "How are you getting on with that science homework? The second part is really hard!"

Jamal "I know what you mean. Here, I've attached some notes from class. Might be helpful."

Narrator Suddenly a light begins to flash red. Someone is trying to hack into Lee and Jamal's chat.

Lee Hey, what's happening?
I didn't write this. Someone's changing my words on screen.

Narrator Jamal goes to find Lee. Together they read the changing text on the screen.

Lee Look! It says I sent this message, "Here are the answers to next week's test." But I didn't!

Narrator More text appears.

Jamal Wait, there's more. It has a message from me saying, "Thanks, Lee. We're going to pass now we have the answers."
No! We didn't write this.
What's going on?

Narrator Jamal tries to change the words but the screen flickers. Then the word 'sharing' flashes up. Their fake online chat is then shared with the whole school – pupils and teachers!

Jamal No!

Lee No!

Narrator Mr McManus appears on the screen.

Jamal Mr McManus, sir. We are not cheating sir, honest. It's Jason sir, he's trying to get us into trouble.

Narrator Mr McManus taps a button on his keyboard. An instant message screen pops up with a picture of Jason.

Mr McManus
Are you involved in this, Jason?

Jason Me sir? No sir! I've only just seen this sir. Cheating on the test! Terrible.

Narrator Jamal and Lee are very angry.

Mr McManus
Jamal says you did this.

Jason How could I, sir?

Jamal Everybody knows he can
do that stuff, sir.
Hacking an online chat
and changing what was said and ...

Narrator Claire's instant message screen pops up.

Claire Sir, Jason was with me studying
for next week's science test ...
unlike *some* people.

Lee But that's not true!

Jason Claire is right, sir.
We've been studying all morning.

Claire Anyway, the whole school knows
about Lee and Jamal. They are
trouble makers ... and now
they are cheats.

Jason Yes sir. And after what they said
about you ... Well, we don't
want anything to do with them.

Mr McManus

I have heard enough! I have
all the proof I need.
Lee, Jamal, I will have to talk
with your parents.

Claire I quite agree, sir.

Jason It's the only way they'll learn.

Claire Can we get back to our studies
now please, sir?

Mr McManus

Yes, of course. Keep up the hard work.

Jason Happy to help, sir.

Narrator Mr McManus presses a button
to end the chat with Jason and Claire.
Then he sends a message to Lee
and Jamal.

Mr McManus
Why can't you two be
more like Jason and Claire?

Lee and Jamal (*together*)
But!

Narrator The screen goes blank.

Jamal This is so unfair. Why us?

Lee I don't think Jason and Claire care who they bully. They just enjoy it.

Jamal They can't get away with cyber-bullying. Somebody has to do something!

Lee You mean us? What can we do?

Jamal Maybe we should talk to them.

Lee You mean ... we should talk with Jason and Claire?

Jamal It's worth a try.
Somebody has to stand up to them.

Lee I suppose ...

Jamal Well, maybe we can get them to confess.

Lee Confess? Fat chance!

Jamal Well, we have to try something!
Maybe if we explain how much trouble they are making, then Jason and Claire will do the right thing.

Lee I don't know if that will work.

Jamal Or we could try and make a deal?

Lee A deal? Like what?

Jamal Oh, I don't know. We just have to try and do something! I don't want detention forever, do you?

Lee Hmm. I suppose we can't make things any worse. Are you going to email them?

Jamal Not likely! They could just do some computer tricks that get us into more trouble.
Let's go round there.

Lee To their house? I suppose we have more chance of changing their minds in person.

Jamal Even if they don't change their minds, well, we can try and get them to tell the truth ... on camera.

Narrator	Jamal picks up an old digital camera and points to the 'record video' button.
Lee	You mean trick them into confessing what they have been doing ... and record it?
Jamal	Exactly! We can clear our names by putting the recording on Yard. Then everybody will know it was Jason and Claire messing around – and not us.

Scene 4

CYBER REVENGE

Narrator Lee and Jamal run over to where Jason and Claire live. They have seen the house on photos on Yard. They creep up to a big window and peep inside.

Jamal Maybe we should just knock on the door and ask to speak to them?

Lee Wait! Did you hear that?

Narrator They hear a lady's voice inside the house call out "Jasey-Poos! Claire-Bear! It's time for your dinner my little darlings."

Jamal 'Jasey-Poos!' 'Claire-Bear!' 'Little darlings!' Surely she can't be talking about Jason and Claire?

Lee Must be! Can you believe she called them little darlings? Big bullies more like.

Jamal Shall we check it out?

Lee Oh yes!

Narrator Just then, Lee and Jamal see Jason and Claire enter the dining room. They sit at the table.

Jason Me first, me first!

Claire No! Me first, me first!

Narrator The twins' mum enters the room and puts bibs on Jason and Claire!

Lee It looks like they're eating baby food.

Jamal No way! And they're wearing bibs!

Lee Ha ha ha. This is *so* funny!
They don't look so tough now!

Jamal Yeah, I guess most bullies
are just big babies like these two.

Lee Yeah. They only pick on others to make themselves look tough.

Jamal I'll get my camera out and start recording. They won't be able to pick on anyone else when people at school see this!

Narrator As Jamal starts filming, a man comes into the room. He is carrying a big stack of school books. He sits at a computer in the corner of the room.

Jamal Look, he's got a load of school books. Maybe he's a teacher.

Lee Not from our school.

Narrator Jason shouts over to the man at the computer.

Jason Can't you do it any quicker?
I need my maths by tomorrow.

Claire Yeah, and I need my history
project too!

Narrator The man sighs and starts tapping
the computer keyboard at an
amazing speed.

Lee I don't get it. What's going on?

Jamal That man is doing Jason and Claire's homework for them!

Lee Why, the little cheats!

Jamal Well, we've got it all on film now. Let's see what Mr McManus thinks about it.

Narrator Jamal keeps filming.

Jason What a shame Lee and Jamal don't have a servant to do their homework for them!

Claire Let's keep playing our cyber tricks on them. They will be in detention for the rest of their lives!

Jason Yeah, McManus looked really angry!
Did you see his face?

Claire Yeah. He's so easy to fool.

Narrator Lee and Jamal look at each other and smile.

Lee Ha ha, this is brilliant!
We have a full confession now.

Jamal Yeah, this proves they are cheats
and that they were hacking
into our online messages.

Lee Everyone will see that they're
not big and tough at all.
They're just spoilt little brats.

Jamal Pinch me, I must be dreaming.
This is going to be *so* good!

Narrator Finally, Jason and Claire's mum comes back. She takes off their bibs and wipes their faces clean.

Lee Well, I think that's enough filming don't you?

Jamal Oh yes! When we upload this bit of film onto Yard, Jason and Claire's bullying days will be over for good!

Lee And we won't be in trouble anymore with Mr McManus!

Jamal Result!

Scene 4 Cyber revenge

In the chatroom ...

You go to the same school as Lee and Jamal.
While you are on Yard, this message comes up from Jason.

You are logged on to: Yard

Sender: Jason

Do you want to see something really funny?

Why not check out the pictures of Lee and Jamal on my website? They look soooo stupid!

They are such losers!

- What do you think about this message? How would you feel if you were Lee or Jamal? Design an anti-bullying poster and include a section on cyber-bullying.

Role play …

Work in a group of three.
Take the parts of Mr McManus, Jason and Claire.

- Think about how the play ends. What do you think will happen next?
- Create a new scene in which Mr McManus calls Jason and Claire into his office.

In pairs …

- *Work with a partner. Think about how Jason and Claire could show they are sorry.*
- *Make a list of your ideas.*
- *Can you write a short scene for the play where the bullies say sorry?*

Tip: As well as talking to Lee and Jamal, the bullies could do something to make up for being so mean.